The Heart of IT Architecture

Beyond Cement, Steel, and Buzzwords

by

Lingaraj Misra

The Heart of IT Architecture

In this book, Lingaraj Misra explores the core principles of IT architecture, offering practical advice and strategies for building systems that are robust, scalable, and adaptable. Whether you are an IT professional, a business leader, or simply curious about the field, this book provides valuable insights to help you navigate the ever-evolving landscape of technology.

The journey of creating an IT architecture is like constructing a grand edifice. Just as a building relies on a strong foundation and thoughtful design, an IT system depends on principles beyond technical specifications. 'Cement' and 'steel' represent foundational elements and structural integrity, but the heart of IT architecture lies in understanding the deeper principles that ensure resilience and adaptability.

I would like to dedicate this book to Sudha, my loving wife, and Aarnav, my wonderful son—your unwavering support, endless love, curiosity, and laughter are my greatest sources of strength and inspiration.

I would also like to extend my heartfelt gratitude to all my mentors and colleagues. Your guidance, wisdom, and encouragement have been invaluable throughout this journey. Thank you for believing in me and helping me grow both personally and professionally.

Content

The Heart of IT Architecture

Welcome to "The Heart of IT Architecture: Beyond Cement, Steel, and Buzzwords." This book isn't just about building systems—it's about building systems that last. As IT professionals, we've all seen it: the allure of shiny tools, the buzz of trendy technologies, and the chaos that ensues when architecture takes a backseat to speed and convenience.

In my journey as an architect, I've witnessed systems that defied expectations, adapting gracefully to years of change. I've also seen systems crumble under the weight of poor planning, overloaded with features no one asked for and incapable of handling what truly mattered. What makes the difference? Thoughtful, sustainable architecture.

This book is a reflection on the lessons learned in IT architecture, shared through the lens of practical advice and relatable analogies. Whether you're a seasoned architect, a developer looking to understand the bigger picture, or a business leader trying to bridge the gap between strategy and technology, this book is for you.

Throughout these pages, you'll find guidance on:

- Creating blueprints that prioritize sustainability over hype.
- Choosing tools that complement your vision rather than distract from it.
- Building foundations that can adapt to change, scale effortlessly, and evolve with your business needs.
- Aligning IT with business goals to ensure every system serves a purpose.

But this book isn't just a technical manual. It's also a reminder to find humor in the chaos, to embrace challenges as opportunities, and to celebrate the wins—no matter how small they may seem.

In IT architecture, as in life, it's not just about the materials—it's about the design. The steel and cement of a system are just building blocks; the real magic happens in the planning, the foresight, and the execution.

Thank you for joining me on this journey into the heart of IT architecture. Together, let's explore what it takes to build systems that don't just meet today's needs but thrive in tomorrow's world.

Warm regards,

Lingaraj Misra

Chapter 1: Welcome to the Construction Zone

Imagine someone hands you an empty plot of land and a pile of bricks. They grin and say, "Build me the perfect house. Oh, and it should withstand earthquakes, double as a skyscraper someday, and have enough charm to make it into a design magazine." Fun, right?

That's what being an IT architect feels like.

In IT, tools like Cloud, AI, and Low Code are your bricks and cement. Everyone's obsessed with them, as if the right tool can magically create a masterpiece. Spoiler alert: it can't. Tools are great, but they're just part of the puzzle.

Without a solid blueprint, all you'll end up with is a very expensive mess.

And that's where IT architecture comes in. It's not about the tools themselves—it's about how you use them to design something sustainable, adaptable, and, most importantly, not a total disaster when things change (because they will change).

Buzzwords Aren't Magic Wands

Let's talk about buzzwords. IT is full of them, and they sound so exciting: "We're implementing AI!" or "Everything's moving to the Cloud!" Cue applause and budget approvals.

But here is the thing: Cloud, AI, Low Code—these are tools, not solutions. Using them without a plan is like buying the fanciest materials for a house but forgetting to build a foundation. Sure, your house looks cool for a minute—until it rains, or someone opens a window too hard.

The point is, no single tool is going to solve all your problems. A hammer is great, but it will not build a house on its own. The same goes for IT. You need a vision and a design to make those tools work together.

What Does an Architect Actually Do?

In short, the IT architect's job is to make sure the "house" does not fall down—no matter how much the occupants complain about the wallpaper.

It's about creating a system that can grow and adapt as the business evolves. Maybe your company starts as a cozy cottage but eventually needs to be a high-rise office. A good architect plans for that from the start. They make sure the foundation is solid and the walls can stretch.

This means thinking long-term. It's not enough to pick the latest tech or follow the trendiest buzzword. You need to ask: Will this work next year? What about five years from now?

The Problem with Overbuilding

Let's say you're building a simple two-bedroom house, but halfway through, someone insists it also needs a helipad, an indoor pool, and a library with secret doors. Sounds awesome, right? Sure, until you realize the whole thing is wildly over budget, behind schedule, and you still don't have a working bathroom.

This happens all the time in IT. Businesses get distracted by what's trendy and forget to focus on what they actually need. Suddenly, you're stuck with a system that looks impressive on paper but doesn't solve any real problems.

A sustainable IT architecture isn't about packing in as much as you can—it's about designing something that works, grows, and stays manageable over time. And that starts with a clear understanding of your actual needs.

Start with the Foundation

Every house starts with a foundation. In IT, your foundation is the core of your architecture: the principles, systems, and frameworks that everything else is built on. And just like in construction, if the foundation isn't solid, it doesn't matter how pretty the walls are—sooner or later, the whole thing will collapse.

This is where a lot of IT projects go wrong. Teams rush to implement the latest tools without considering whether their foundation can support them. It's like putting a three-story mansion on top of a cardboard box—flashy, but doomed.

To avoid this, you need to ask yourself:

- What's essential for our system to function today?
- What will we need to scale in the future?
- Are we building something flexible enough to handle changes down the road?

The House That Never Stops Growing

Here's a fun fact about IT systems: They're never "done."

In construction, you can eventually step back, hand over the keys, and say, "Here's your house!" In IT, it doesn't work that way. Business requirements change, new technologies emerge, and suddenly, your once-perfect system feels outdated.

That's why IT architecture is all about adaptability. It's not enough to build for today—you have to design for tomorrow, next year, and beyond. Think of your IT system as a house that needs to grow with its occupants. Maybe today it's a cozy cottage, but one day it might need to be a skyscraper. Your job is to make sure the foundation can handle that growth.

The Architect's Mindset

So, how do you approach IT architecture without losing your mind? Start by focusing on clarity and simplicity.

A good IT architect doesn't try to cram every trend into their design. They think critically, plan strategically, and always keep the big picture in mind.

Remember, you're not just building a system—you're creating something that supports your business, adapts to change, and makes life easier for the people who use it. If you can do that, congratulations—you're already ahead of the game.

The Heart of IT Architecture

Chapter 2: Bricks, Cement, and Buzzwords

If buzzwords were bricks, IT architects would have enough material to build the Great Wall of China five times over. Every year, there's a new crop of trendy terms that everyone's talking about: Cloud, AI, Blockchain, Low Code, and whatever next year's big thing will be. It's easy to get swept up in the excitement—after all, these tools sound promising, don't they?

Here's the thing, though: buzzwords don't build systems. They're just tools. And like any tools, they're only as good as the person using them. Imagine a contractor showing up to build your house, bragging about their fancy new hammer. "This hammer is amazing," they say, waving it around. "It's going to revolutionize your home!" Meanwhile, there's no blueprint in sight, and they've already started hammering nails into thin air.

Sounds ridiculous, right? Yet in IT, this happens all the time.

The Buzzword Bubble

Let's take a closer look at some of the buzzwords that have dominated IT conversations over the years:

Cloud: Everyone's in the Cloud these days—or at least claims to be. But what does that actually mean? Are you leveraging the

Cloud in a way that adds value, or are you just storing files on someone else's computer?

AI: Artificial intelligence sounds futuristic, but it's not going to run your business for you. At best, it can help automate some processes or provide insights—if you know how to use it.

Blockchain: The darling of buzzwords. Perfect for cryptocurrency, but do you really need a decentralized ledger for your HR system? Probably not.

Low Code: The promise of software development for everyone. But spoiler alert: if you don't know what you're building, even the easiest tool won't save you.

Each of these technologies has potential, but none of them are magic solutions. The real magic lies in how you integrate them into a coherent system that solves real problems.

Tools vs. Architecture

Let's get one thing straight: tools are just the building blocks. They're the cement, steel, and bricks of your IT system. The architecture is the blueprint that tells you how to use those materials. And the difference between the two? Night and day.

Think of it like this: You can have the fanciest bricks in the world, but if you don't know how to lay them, you'll just end up with a very expensive pile. Architecture isn't about having the best tools— it's about using the right tools in the right way.

This is where a lot of IT projects go off the rails. Businesses get so caught up in buzzwords that they forget to ask, "Do we even need this?" They invest in tools they don't understand, for problems they don't have, and then wonder why their systems are a tangled mess.

The Dangers of Shiny Object Syndrome

Let's be honest: who doesn't love shiny new things? IT teams are no different. Every time a new tool hits the market, there's a rush to adopt it—often without much thought about how it fits into the bigger picture.

But here's the reality: just because a tool is shiny and new doesn't mean it's right for your business. Imagine adding a skylight to a house with no roof or installing a state-of-the-art sound system in a building with no electricity. It might look impressive, but it is not going to work.

The same goes for IT. Before you adopt a new tool, ask yourself:

- Does it solve a real problem?
- Does it align with our architecture?
- Can we maintain it long-term?

If the answer to any of these questions is "no," it's probably not the right fit.

Buzzwords Are Not the Enemy

Now, don't get me wrong buzzwords aren't inherently bad. They reflect innovation, and many of them represent valuable tools and technologies. But the key is to approach them with a critical eye.

A good IT architect does not chase trends—they evaluate them. They look beyond the hype and ask, "How does this fit into our overall strategy? Does it make sense for us?"

Because at the end of the day, it is not about having the fanciest tools. It is about building something that works, something that lasts, and something that adds real value to your business.

Putting It All Together

So, what is the takeaway here? Buzzwords might sound exciting, but they are not the heart of IT architecture. Your job is to look past the hype and focus on the bigger picture. Think strategically, plan carefully, and remember that the best systems are not built on trends—they are built on a solid foundation.

In the next chapter, we will dive deeper into what it means to create that foundation, and how you can ensure your architecture is built to last. Spoiler alert: it is not about using more buzzwords.

Chapter 3: Blueprints vs. Chaos

Every great structure starts with a blueprint. In IT architecture, the blueprint is your plan—a roadmap for what you are building, how it will work, and how it will grow. Sounds simple enough, right? And yet, it is amazing how many IT projects skip this step entirely.

Instead of a clear, detailed plan, many teams dive straight into implementation. They start piecing together tools, technologies, and features without asking, "What are we actually trying to build?" The result? Chaos.

The Importance of a Blueprint

Let's take a step back. Imagine you're building a house. Would you start construction without a plan? Would you just start pouring concrete, hammering nails, and hoping for the best? Of course not. You'd create a blueprint first—a detailed design showing everything from the foundation to the roof.

IT architecture is no different. Without a clear blueprint, you're flying blind. You might end up with something that works for a while, but sooner or later, cracks will start to show. Systems won't integrate properly, performance will suffer, and scaling will become a nightmare.

What Happens Without a Blueprint?

Here's what happens when you skip the planning phase: Integration Issues: Your systems don't talk to each other. Instead of a seamless flow of data, you get a patchwork of disconnected tools and processes.

- Performance Problems: Without a well-thought-out design, your system might struggle to oversee the demands placed on it. Bottlenecks and crashes become all too common.
- Scalability Challenges: A poorly planned system

might work fine today, but what happens.

- When your business grows? Without a scalable architecture, you'll hit a wall—and fixing it won't be cheap.

- Skipping the blueprint is not just risky—it's costly. The time and money you save upfront will be nothing compared to the expense of fixing a broken system later.

Building a Solid Plan

So, how do you create a blueprint for your IT architecture? Start by asking the right questions:

What are your goals? What is this system supposed to achieve?

What problems are you solving? Who will use it? Consider the needs of your users—both technical and non-technical.

How will it grow? Think about the future. What will your business look like in 1 year? 5 years?

A good blueprint does not just outline what you're building—it also considers how you'll maintain and adapt it over time. Flexibility is key.

The Role of Collaboration

One of the biggest mistakes teams make is treating the blueprint as an IT-only document. But IT architecture does not exist in a vacuum—it supports your business. That is why it's crucial to collaborate with stakeholders across your organization. Bring in voices from every department. Talk to end-users, managers, and executives. Understand their needs, challenges, and priorities. The more perspectives you include, the stronger your blueprint will be.

From Chaos to Clarity

Here is the good news: even if your IT system feels chaotic today, it's never too late to introduce structure. Start by stepping back and creating a plan. Identify what's working, what's not, and where you need to go next. Remember, architecture isn't about perfection—it's about direction. With a clear blueprint, you can turn even the messiest system into something sustainable and effective.

In the next chapter, we will explore how to build strong foundations that support your architecture for the long haul. Spoiler: it is all about getting the basics right.

Chapter 4: Foundations First

Before you start building walls, hanging chandeliers, or installing the latest high-tech gadgets, there is one thing you absolutely need: a sturdy foundation. In both construction and IT, the foundation is what holds everything together. Get it wrong, and the fanciest tools and features will not save you.

In IT architecture, your foundation is the core of your system—the basic elements that everything else depends on. This includes your infrastructure, data architecture, and the principles that guide your design. A solid foundation ensures stability, scalability, and security.

Why Foundations Matter

Let us look at a simple analogy. Imagine building a house on loose sand. No matter how beautiful the design, no matter how expensive the materials, that house will not last long. It'll start to sink, crack, and eventually collapse.

The same goes for IT. If your architecture is not built on a solid foundation, it won't be able to handle growth, change, or the unexpected demands of the future. Stability comes first.

The Key Elements of a Strong Foundation

1. **Infrastructure:** Your servers, networks, and cloud environments are the backbone of your architecture. Invest in reliable, scalable infrastructure that can grow with your business.

2. **Data Architecture:** Data is the lifeblood of modern IT systems. A well-organized data architecture ensures your information is accessible, secure, and easy to integrate across systems.

3. **Security:** No foundation is complete without robust security measures. Think of security as the locks and alarms on your house— it keeps your assets safe.

4. **Design Principles:** Establish clear principles to guide your

architecture. For example, prioritize modularity, scalability, and simplicity. These principles act as guardrails to keep your system on track.

What Happens Without a Strong Foundation?

Without a solid foundation, your IT architecture is vulnerable to a host of problems:

- Performance Issues: Systems may crash or slow down under heavy load.
- Integration Failures: Components don't work well together, leading to inefficiencies.

- Security Risks: Weak foundations are easy targets for cyberattacks.

- High Maintenance Costs: Fixing a poorly built system can be time-consuming and expensive.

Building for the Future

A solid foundation is not just about today—it's about the future. Ask yourself:

- Can this system scale as my business grows?

- Will it be easy to adapt to innovative technologies and requirements?

- Is it secure enough to protect my data and operations?

By addressing these questions upfront, you are setting yourself up for long-term success.

Learning from Real-World Failures

History is full of examples of systems that failed due to weak foundations. From high-profile data breaches to systems that could not handle growth, the lessons are clear: investing in a strong foundation pays off.

As an IT architect, it is your job to ensure the foundation is solid before moving forward. This means being proactive, asking the hard questions, and sometimes saying "no" to features that compromise the integrity of the system.

In the next chapter, we will look at how to choose the right tools and technologies—the "bricks and mortar" of your architecture. But remember, no matter how fancy the bricks, they are only as strong as the foundation beneath them.

Chapter 5: Tools That Build or Break

When it comes to IT architecture, tools can be your best friends—or your worst enemies. The right tools, used the right way, can help you build systems that are efficient, scalable, and sustainable. The wrong tools, or even the right tools used poorly, can create a tangled mess that is impossible to manage.

In this chapter, we will explore the role tools play in IT architecture. We will look at how to choose the right tools, use them effectively, and avoid the pitfalls that can derail even the best-laid plans.

The Role of Tools in IT Architecture

Tools are the building blocks of your IT system. They include everything from programming languages and frameworks to databases, cloud platforms, and integration tools. But here is the catch: tools are just that—tools. They are not solutions. They do not solve problems on their own; they need to be wielded by someone who knows how to use them.

A hammer is great for driving nails, but it will not help you install a window. Similarly, a powerful database management system is useless if you do not understand your data requirements.

Choosing the Right Tools

Selecting the right tools for your architecture is a critical step. Here are some factors to consider:

1. Alignment with Goals: Does the tool support your business objectives? For example, if you are building a real-time analytics platform, you will need tools that can process large volumes of data quickly.

2. Ease of Integration: Can the tool integrate seamlessly with your existing systems? Compatibility is key to ensuring everything works together smoothly.

3. Scalability: Will the tool be able to handle your system's growth? A tool that works for a small project might struggle with larger workloads.

4. Community and Support: Does the tool have a strong community of users and developers? A tool with robust support is less likely to leave you stranded when you hit a roadblock.

5. Cost: Is the tool within your budget? Remember to consider not just the upfront cost, but also the cost of maintenance and upgrades.

The Danger of Shiny Objects

It is easy to get distracted by the latest and greatest tools. Every year, new technologies hit the market, promising to revolutionize the way we work. But just because a tool is new does not mean it's the right fit for your system.

Avoid the trap of chasing trends. Instead, focus on finding tools that meet your specific needs. Ask yourself:

- Does this tool solve a problem we have?
- Is it better than the tools we are currently using?
- Can we justify the cost and effort of switching?

Using Tools Effectively

Once you've chosen the right tools, the next step is to use them effectively. This means understanding their strengths and limitations and using them in ways that maximize their value.

1. Training and Expertise: Make sure your team knows how to use the tools properly. Invest in training and encourage knowledge sharing.

2. Best Practices: Follow industry best practices for using each tool. This can help you avoid common mistakes and get the most out of your investment.

3. Monitoring and Optimization: Regularly monitor how the tools are performing and look for opportunities to optimize their use. For example, you might discover that tweaking a database query can significantly improve performance.

4. Documentation: Keep detailed documentation on how the tools are used in your system. This makes it easier to troubleshoot problems and onboard new team members.

When Tools Become a Liability

Even the best tools can become liabilities if they're not managed properly. Here are some common pitfalls to watch out for:

1. Tool Overload: Using too many tools can create unnecessary complexity. Stick to a streamlined set of tools that meet your needs.

2. Lack of Standardization: If different teams use different tools, it can create silos and make it harder to collaborate. Establish standards for which tools should be used for specific tasks.

3. Vendor Lock-In: Be cautious about becoming overly reliant on a single vendor. Look for tools that support open standards and interoperability.

4. Neglecting Maintenance: Tools need regular updates and maintenance to stay secure and effective. Don't let your tools fall behind.

Let's look at some real-world examples of tools that build or break IT systems:

1. Success Story: During my tenure as the IT Architect of a global logistics company, we faced significant challenges integrating our numerous legacy systems. Each department operated in silos, leading to inefficiencies and frequent errors. We decided to implement a sophisticated data integration platform as Eka. This platform seamlessly connected our disparate systems, enabling real-time data flow across the organization. The results were remarkable: operational efficiency soared, error rates plummeted, and customer satisfaction improved dramatically. The platform's flexibility allowed us to scale and adapt quickly to market demands, positioning us as a leader in the logistics industry.

2. **Cautionary Tale:** Recently I consulted for a promising startup in the fintech sector. Eager to stay ahead of the curve, hoping it would revolutionize their predictive analytics capabilities. However, without a deep understanding of the platform's complexities and without sufficient expertise in AI, the implementation turned into a nightmare. The system became

overly intricate, hard to maintain, and ultimately, the team struggled to extract meaningful insights. After months of frustration and resource drain, the project was abandoned, and the company reverted to simpler, more manageable solutions.

These examples highlight the importance of choosing the right tools and using them wisely.

The Architect's Role

As an IT architect, your job is to guide the selection and use of tools. This means staying informed about the latest technologies, evaluating their potential, and making decisions based on what is best for your system.

Remember, tools are enablers—they are not the star of the show. The real magic lies in how you bring them together to create something greater than the sum of its parts.

Looking Ahead

In the next chapter, we will explore the concept of sustainability in IT architecture. How do you build systems that can adapt and thrive in a constantly changing environment? Stay tuned for practical insights and strategies.

Chapter 6: Sustainability: The Secret Sauce

Sustainability might not sound as exciting as buzzwords like "AI" or "Blockchain," but in IT architecture, it's the secret sauce that keeps your systems running smoothly long after the initial hype fades. Sustainability is not just about reducing costs or minimizing waste; it's about creating systems that can adapt, grow, and thrive over time.

In this chapter, we will dive into the principles of sustainability in IT architecture. We will explore why it matters, how to achieve it, and what happens when it's ignored.

Why Sustainability Matters

IT systems are never truly "finished." Businesses evolve, markets change, and technology advances at a dizzying pace. A system that works perfectly today might become a liability tomorrow if it cannot keep up with new demands.

Sustainability ensures that your architecture remains relevant and effective, no matter what the future holds.

It is about building systems that,

Adapt to Change: Whether it is a new technology, a shift in business strategy, or a sudden spike in demand, sustainable systems can handle change with grace.

Minimize Technical Debt: Poorly designed systems can accumulate technical debt—shortcuts and compromises that make future updates more difficult and costly.

Support Long-Term Goals: Sustainable systems align with your organization's long-term objectives, rather than just addressing immediate needs.

The Principles of Sustainable IT Architecture-

To build sustainable systems, focus on these core principles:

1. Modularity: Design your system as a collection of independent modules that can be updated or replaced without affecting the entire system. This makes it easier to adapt to new requirements or technologies.

2. Scalability: Ensure your system can handle growth—whether it's more users, more data, or more complexity. Scalability is the key to staying ahead of demand.

3. Interoperability: Use open standards and APIs to ensure your system can integrate with other tools and platforms. Avoid proprietary solutions that lock you into a single vendor.

4. Simplicity: Complexity is the enemy of sustainability. Keep your architecture as simple as possible while still meeting your needs.

5. Documentation: A well-documented system is easier to maintain and update. Invest time in creating clear, comprehensive documentation for your architecture.

The Cost of Ignoring Sustainability

What happens when sustainability isn't a priority? Let's look at some common pitfalls:

1.   **Fragile Systems:** Without sustainability, systems become brittle and prone to failure. Even minor changes can cause major disruptions.

2.   **Skyrocketing Maintenance Costs:** Unsustainable systems require constant fixes and patches, draining time and resources.

3. **Missed Opportunities:** If your system cannot adapt quickly, you may miss out on new opportunities—whether it's a market trend, a technological breakthrough, or a business expansion.

4. **Frustrated Teams:** Developers and IT teams often bear the brunt of unsustainable systems, facing

endless workarounds and mounting technical debt.

Strategies for Building Sustainability

So, how do you create systems that stand the test of time? Here are some practical strategies:

1. Plan for the Future: Think beyond today's requirements. Anticipate future needs and design your system to accommodate them.

2. Embrace Automation: Automate repetitive tasks like testing, deployment, and monitoring. This reduces errors, saves time, and ensures consistency.

3. Monitor and Optimize: Regularly monitor your system's performance and look for ways to improve it. Sustainability isn't a one-time effort—it's an ongoing process.

4. Invest in Training: Equip your team with the skills they need to maintain and improve your system. A well-trained team is critical to sustainability.

5. Foster Collaboration: Encourage collaboration between IT and business teams. A shared understanding of goals and priorities ensures your architecture supports the broader organization.

Real-World Examples

Let's take a look at some real-world examples of sustainability in action:

1. The Success Story: While overseeing IT architecture of a global retailer designed, I have seen its e-commerce platform with modularity and scalability in mind. When the pandemic caused a surge in online shopping, the platform scaled effortlessly, supporting record-breaking sales without a hitch.

2. The Warning Tale: A mid-sized company ignored sustainability and built its systems with proprietary tools. When the vendor discontinued support, the company was forced to rebuild its

entire architecture from scratch—a costly and time-consuming process.

These examples highlight the importance of thinking long-term and prioritizing sustainability from the start.

The Architect's Role

As an IT architect, sustainability should be at the core of everything you do. Your role isn't just to design systems that work today—it's to design systems that will continue to work tomorrow, next year, and beyond.

This means balancing immediate needs with long-term goals, making thoughtful decisions about tools and technologies, and advocating for sustainability at every stage of the process.

Looking Ahead

In the next chapter, we'll explore how to align IT architecture with business goals. After all, a sustainable system is only valuable if it supports the success of the organization it serves.

Chapter 7: When Business Meets Blueprints

The ultimate goal of IT architecture isn't just to build systems that work—it's to build systems that work for the business. Without alignment between IT and business goals, even the most technically impressive architecture can end up as a costly, underutilized investment.

In this chapter, we'll explore the importance of aligning IT architecture with business objectives. We'll discuss how to bridge the gap between technical teams and stakeholders, and how to ensure your architecture delivers real value to the organization.

Why Alignment Matters?

Think of IT and business as two sides of the same coin. One can't succeed without the other. IT provides the tools and systems that enable the business to operate, grow, and innovate. The business provides the vision, goals, and resources that drive IT.

When IT and business goals are aligned, the results can be transformative. Systems are designed with purpose, projects are completed on time and within budget, and teams work together toward a common goal. But when there's a disconnect, it's a different story: miscommunication, wasted resources, and systems that fail to deliver value.

Common Challenges

Aligning IT architecture with business goals isn't always easy. Here are some common challenges:

1. Lack of Communication: IT teams and business stakeholders often speak different languages. Without clear communication, it's easy for goals to get lost in translation.

2. Conflicting Priorities: IT might prioritize technical excellence, while the business focuses on speed and cost. Balancing these priorities is crucial.

3. Changing Requirements: Business needs can evolve rapidly, leaving IT struggling to keep up.

4. Limited Understanding: Business leaders may not fully understand the potential of IT, while IT teams may lack insight into the business strategy.

Bridging the Gap

To align IT architecture with business goals, focus on building strong relationships and fostering collaboration between teams. Here is how:

1. Start with the Why: Before diving into technical details, ensure everyone understands the purpose of the project. What business problem are you solving? What are the desired outcomes?

2. Involve Stakeholders Early: Engage business leaders and end-users in the planning process. Their input can help ensure the architecture meets real-world needs.

3. Translate Technical Jargon: Avoid overwhelming stakeholders with technical jargon. Use clear, simple language to explain how the architecture supports business objectives.

4. Establish Priorities Together: Work with stakeholders to identify priorities and constraints. This ensures the architecture is both technically sound and aligned with business needs.

5. Create a Feedback Loop: Regularly gather feedback from stakeholders to ensure the architecture remains aligned with evolving goals.

Metrics for Success

How do you know if your architecture is delivering value to the business? Use metrics to measure success. These might include:

Operational Efficiency: Has the architecture improved productivity or reduced costs?

Customer Satisfaction: Are customers benefiting from faster, more reliable systems?

Business Growth: Has the architecture enabled new opportunities, such as entering new markets or launching new products?

Scalability: Can the system support future growth without significant redesigns?

Real-World Examples

Let's look at some examples of IT architecture aligning—or failing to align—with business goals:

1. The Win: A financial services company revamped its IT systems to support digital banking. By aligning the architecture with the business goal of enhancing customer experience, they increased user retention and attracted new clients.

2. The Misstep: A retail chain invested heavily in a cutting-edge inventory system but failed to consult store managers during the design phase. The system did not meet their needs, leading to low adoption and wasted resources.

These examples highlight the importance of collaboration and alignment in creating successful IT architecture.

The Architect's Role

The Heart of IT Architecture

As an IT architect, you are the bridge between technology and business. Your role is to ensure that every decision—whether it is choosing a tool, designing a system, or prioritizing a feature— is made with the business in mind.

This requires more than technical expertise. It requires communication, empathy, and a deep understanding of the organization's goals. By aligning IT architecture with business objectives, you can deliver systems that not only work, but also drive success.

Looking Ahead

In the next chapter, we will explore the ongoing process of maintaining and improving IT architecture. How do you keep your systems running smoothly while adapting to change? Stay tuned for practical strategies and insights.

Chapter 8: Maintenance and Renovation

IT architecture, much like a well-loved home, needs regular upkeep. Over time, systems can become outdated, overloaded, or simply inefficient as new technologies emerge, and business needs evolve. This chapter dives into the ongoing process of maintaining and renovating IT architecture to keep it relevant and efficient.

Why Maintenance Matters?

Imagine a house where the roof has not been checked in years, the plumbing is leaking, and the foundation is beginning to crack. You can still live in it—barely—but it is only a matter of time before something critical fails.

In IT, neglected systems can lead to performance issues, security vulnerabilities, and rising maintenance costs. Regular maintenance ensures that your architecture remains stable, secure, and aligned with current needs.

The Signs of a System in Need

How do you know when your IT architecture needs attention? Here are some common signs:

1. Slow Performance: Systems

that were once fast and responsive start to lag under increased workloads.

2. Integration Challenges: New tools or features are difficult to implement because the architecture wasn't designed for flexibility.

3. Rising Costs: Maintenance and operational costs keep increasing without noticeable improvements.

4. User Complaints: End-users report frequent errors, slowdowns, or difficulty using the system.

5. Security Risks: Outdated components make your system vulnerable to cyberattacks.

Recognizing these signs early

allows you to address issues before they escalate into major problems.

Strategies for Effective Maintenance

1. Regular Audits: Conduct regular audits to identify weak points, inefficiencies, or outdated components in your architecture. This proactive approach helps prevent larger issues down the road.

2. Automated Monitoring: Implement tools that monitor system performance, security, and usage in real time. Automation can help you spot and address issues quickly.

3. Documentation Updates: Keep documentation up to date. This makes it easier to troubleshoot problems, onboard new team members, and plan future changes.

4. Prioritize Security: Regularly update and patch your systems to protect against evolving threats. Security should always be a top priority.

5. Stakeholder Feedback: Engage with users and stakeholders to understand their pain points and priorities. Their insights can guide your maintenance efforts.

When to Renovate?

Sometimes, maintenance isn't enough. If your architecture is fundamentally flawed or unable to meet future demands, it may be time for a renovation—or even a complete rebuild.

Here are some scenarios where renovation makes sense: Technological Obsolescence: Key components of your system are no longer supported by vendors or compatible with modern tools. Scalability Limitations: Your architecture can't handle increased traffic, data, or complexity.

High Technical Debt: Years of quick fixes and workarounds have made the system difficult to manage or improve.

Business Transformation: Significant changes in your business model or strategy require a different approach to IT.

Planning a Renovation

Renovating IT architecture is no small task. It requires careful planning and execution to avoid disruptions and ensure a successful outcome. Here's how to approach it:

1. Define Clear Goals: What are you trying to achieve with the renovation? Be specific about your objectives, whether it's improved performance, lower costs, or better scalability.

2. Engage Stakeholders: Include input from all relevant parties—IT teams, business leaders, and end-users—to ensure the renovation meets everyone's needs.

3. Create a Roadmap: Break the renovation into manageable phases. This minimizes disruption and allows you to evaluate progress along the way.

4. Test Thoroughly: Before deploying any changes, test them in a controlled environment to identify and fix potential issues.

5. Communicate Clearly: Keep stakeholders informed throughout the process. Transparency builds trust and helps manage expectations.

Balancing Maintenance and Innovation

One of the biggest challenges in IT is finding the right balance between maintaining existing systems and investing in new technologies. Here are some tips for striking that balance:

Allocate Resources Wisely: Divide your budget and team resources between maintenance and innovation. Avoid neglecting one for the other.

Adopt a "Fix It Forward" Approach: Address issues in a way that supports future growth. For example, when updating a legacy system, consider how the changes can pave the way for modernization.

Embrace Continuous Improvement: View maintenance and renovation as ongoing processes rather than one-time projects.

Learning from Real-World Examples

1. A Proactive Approach: A healthcare provider implemented regular audits and automated monitoring tools to maintain its IT systems. As a result, they avoided major outages and consistently met regulatory requirements.

2. The Cost of Neglect: A retail company delayed renovating its outdated e-commerce platform. When a surge in traffic caused the system to crash during a holiday sale, they lost revenue and customer trust.

These examples highlight the importance of proactive maintenance and timely renovation.

The Architect's Role

As an IT architect, you're the custodian of the system's health. Your role is to ensure that maintenance is prioritized, renovations are well-planned, and the architecture remains a valuable asset to the organization.

Looking Ahead

In the next chapter, we will explore how IT architects can develop the skills and mindset needed to excel in their roles. From technical expertise to communication and leadership, we will cover what it takes to succeed in this dynamic field.

Chapter 9: The Architect's Toolkit

Being an IT architect isn't just about technical know-how—it's about having the right tools in your metaphorical toolkit. From technical skills and design principles to communication and leadership, an effective architect blends a variety of capabilities to excel in their role.

In this chapter, we will break down the essential skills and tools every IT architect needs. Whether you are a seasoned professional or just starting out, these insights will help you elevate your craft.

Technical Expertise

At its core, IT architecture is a technical discipline. To design systems that work, you need a deep understanding of the technologies involved. Here are some areas where technical expertise is critical:

1. Infrastructure Knowledge: Understand the building blocks of IT systems, including servers, networks, and cloud platforms.

2. Programming and Development: While you don't need to be a developer, familiarity with programming languages and frameworks helps you make informed decisions about tools and integrations.

3. Data Architecture: Know how to design systems that handle data efficiently and securely. This includes database design, data flow, and analytics.

4. Security Best Practices: Security is non-negotiable. Stay up-to-date on the latest threats and solutions to ensure your systems are protected.

5. Emerging Technologies: Keep an eye on trends like AI, IoT, and blockchain. Even if they're not relevant today, they may shape the future of IT architecture.

Design Principles

Great architecture is built on solid design principles. These principles guide your decisions and ensure your systems are scalable, maintainable, and effective. Key principles include:

1. Modularity: Design systems as a collection of independent modules that can be updated or replaced without affecting the whole system.

2. Scalability: Build systems that can handle growth—whether it's more users, more data, or new features.

3. Simplicity: Complexity is the enemy of good design. Aim for solutions that are as simple as possible while still meeting requirements.

4. Interoperability: Use open standards and APIs to ensure your systems can integrate with others.

5. Flexibility: Design with change in mind. Systems should be easy to adapt as needs evolve.

Communication Skills

Technical skills are important, but they're not enough. As an architect, you're the bridge between technical teams and business stakeholders. This requires excellent communication skills:

1. Listening: Understand the needs, goals, and concerns of stakeholders before proposing solutions.

2. Translation: Translate technical concepts into language that non-technical audiences can understand.

3. Negotiation: Balance competing priorities, such as cost, speed, and functionality, to find solutions that work for everyone.

4. Documentation: Create clear, comprehensive documentation that guides teams and provides a reference for future work.

Leadership and Collaboration

IT architects often take on leadership roles, guiding teams and influencing decisions across the organization. Key leadership skills include:

1. **Vision:** Develop a clear vision for your architecture and communicate it effectively to others.

2. **Collaboration:** Work closely with teams across the organization, including developers, operations, and business stakeholders.

3. **Decision-Making:** Make informed decisions quickly and confidently, even in the face of uncertainty.

4. **Mentorship:** Share your knowledge and experience with others, helping to develop the

next generation of IT professionals.

The Tools of the Trade

In addition to skills, IT architects rely on a variety of tools to do their jobs. These tools include:

1. Modeling Software: Tools like ArchiMate and Visio help you create diagrams and blueprints for your architecture.

2. Monitoring Tools: Use tools like Nagios, Splunk, or AWS CloudWatch to monitor system performance and identify issues.

3. Collaboration Platforms: Platforms like Jira, Confluence, and Slack enable communication and project management.

4. Version Control Systems: Tools like Git ensure that changes to code and configurations are tracked and manageable.

5. Educational Resources: Stay sharp by reading industry blogs, attending conferences, and taking online courses.

Continuous Learning

The field of IT architecture is constantly evolving. To stay ahead, commit to lifelong learning. This includes:

1. Staying Curious: Explore new technologies and approaches, even if they're outside your current focus.

2. Networking: Connect with other professionals to share insights and learn from their experiences.

3. Certifications: Consider earning certifications like TOGAF, AWS Solutions Architect, or Cisco Certified Architect to validate your skills.

4. Feedback: Seek feedback from peers, teams, and stakeholders to identify areas for improvement.

The Architect's Mindset

Ultimately, being a successful IT architect is about more than just tools and skills—it's about mindset. Approach your work with curiosity, creativity, and a commitment to excellence.

Embrace challenges as opportunities to gain experience and grow.

Looking Ahead

In the final chapter, we'll bring everything together and explore how to future-proof your IT architecture. From anticipating trends to fostering a culture of innovation, we'll discuss how to ensure your systems remain valuable for years to come.

Chapter 10: Designing for Tomorrow

The world of IT is always evolving, and so must your architecture. Building systems for today's needs is important, but the challenge—and opportunity—lies in designing for tomorrow. Future-proofing your IT architecture is not about predicting the future; it's about creating systems that can adapt to whatever comes next.

In this final chapter, we'll explore how to design IT systems that are resilient, flexible, and ready to support innovation for years to come.

The Nature of Change

Change is the only constant in technology. From new tools and platforms to shifting business strategies, IT systems must navigate a constantly changing landscape. Successful architects embrace this reality and build systems that can evolve alongside it.

To future-proof your architecture, start by asking these questions:

1. What trends are shaping the industry?

2. How might business goals evolve in the coming years?

3. What risks or disruptions could impact the system?

Key Principles for Futureproofing

1. **Adaptability:** Design systems that can easily accommodate changes in scale, technology, and functionality. Use modular architectures to enable quick updates and upgrades.

2. **Scalability:** Ensure your systems can handle growth without significant redesigns. This includes supporting more users, more data, and more complexity.

3. **Interoperability:** Use open standards and APIs to ensure your systems can integrate with other tools and platforms, both now and in the future.

4. **Resilience:** Build systems that can recover quickly from failures or disruptions. This includes

redundancy, failover mechanisms, and robust security measures.

5. Sustainability: Consider the long-term impact of your decisions, from environmental sustainability to minimizing technical debt.

Anticipating Trends

While it's impossible to predict the future with certainty, keeping an eye on trends can help you stay ahead. Here are some areas to watch:

1. Artificial Intelligence and Machine Learning: These technologies are transforming industries, from healthcare to finance. Consider how they might impact your systems.

2. Edge Computing: With the rise of IoT devices, edge computing is becoming increasingly important for processing data closer to its source.

3. Hybrid and Multi-Cloud Strategies: Organizations are moving away from single-vendor cloud solutions to hybrid and multi-cloud environments.

4. Cybersecurity: As threats evolve, so must your security measures. Stay proactive in protecting your systems and data.

5. Sustainability Initiatives: Companies are prioritizing green IT practices. Explore how your architecture can contribute to these goals.

The Role of Innovation

Future-proofing isn't just about keeping up—it's about driving innovation. Encourage a culture of experimentation and continuous improvement. This includes:

Piloting New Technologies: Test emerging tools and platforms to see how they might add value.

Encouraging Collaboration: Foster cross-functional teams to generate fresh ideas and perspectives.

Investing in Education: Equip your team with the skills and

knowledge needed to embrace change.

Real-World Examples

1. The Innovator: A tech company built its architecture on modular microservices, enabling it to quickly adopt new tools and features as they became available. This flexibility gave them a competitive edge in a fast-moving market.

2. The Resistor: A traditional enterprise clung to its legacy systems, avoiding updates and innovation. Over time, they struggled to compete with more

agile competitors and faced mounting technical debt.

These stories highlight the importance of building systems that are not just functional, but forward-thinking.

Practical Steps for Future-Proofing

1. Start Small: You don't have to overhaul everything at once. Begin with pilot projects or incremental updates to test new ideas.

2. Involve Stakeholders: Collaborate with business leaders, developers, and end-users to ensure your architecture supports long-term goals.

3. Document Decisions: Keep detailed records of architectural decisions and their rationale. This provides valuable context for future changes.

4. Review Regularly: Periodically assess your architecture to identify areas for improvement and ensure it remains aligned with business needs.

The Architect's Legacy

As an IT architect, your work has a lasting impact on the organization. The systems you design today will shape how the business operates, innovates, and grows in the future.

By focusing on adaptability, resilience, and sustainability, you can leave a legacy of success.

Final Thoughts

IT architecture is as much an art as it is a science. It requires a balance of technical expertise, strategic thinking, and creative problem-solving. By embracing change, fostering collaboration, and always keeping the bigger picture in mind, you can build systems that not only meet today's needs but also pave the way for tomorrow's opportunities.

Thank you for joining this journey through the heart of IT architecture. Now, it's your turn to design something extraordinary.

Conclusion

As we close the pages of *The Heart of IT Architecture: Beyond Cement, Steel, and Buzzwords,* it's clear that IT architecture is more than just a technical discipline—it's a strategic, creative, and forward-thinking craft. It's about turning a pile of tools, technologies, and requirements into systems that truly serve their purpose, not just for today but for the future.

Throughout this book, we've explored the foundations of sustainable IT architecture. From crafting detailed blueprints and choosing the right tools to aligning with business goals and preparing for the unknown, every chapter emphasized the importance of intentionality and adaptability. Architecture isn't about chasing trends or relying on buzzwords—it's about designing systems that solve real problems and empower businesses to thrive.

We've laughed at the pitfalls of "shiny object syndrome" and marveled at the success stories of scalable, modular, and innovative designs. But above all, this book has been a reminder that good architecture isn't just about technical excellence—it's about people, collaboration, and creating something greater than the sum of its parts.

As you move forward in your journey, remember that the heart of IT architecture lies in its ability to evolve, to bridge gaps, and to endure. Keep asking the right questions, thinking strategically, and challenging yourself to build systems that leave a legacy of resilience and success.

Thank you for embarking on this journey. The tools, insights, and principles you now have are just the beginning. The real magic happens when you bring them to life in your own projects, creating IT systems that do not just meet expectations—they redefine them.

Here's to building the future, one sustainable system at a time.

Thank you for taking the time to read my work. Your support means the world to me, and I hope to continue bringing stories that inspire, entertain, and provoke thought.

Warm regards,

Lingaraj Misra

www.ingramcontent.com/pod-product-compliance
Lightning Source LLC
Chambersburg PA
CBHW041338120726
48005CB00014B/2307